MAN VERSUS MOUNTAIN

MOUNT FUJI

Amie Jane Leavitt

PURPLE TOAD PUBLISHING

P.O. Box 631
Kennett Square, Pennsylvania 19348
www.purpletoadpublishing.com

K2 in Kashmir

Kilimanjaro

Mount Everest

Mount Fuji

Mount Olympus

PUBLISHER'S NOTE: The data in this book has been researched in depth, and to the best of our knowledge is factual. Although every measure is taken to give an accurate account, Purple Toad Publishing makes no warranty of the accuracy of the information and is not liable for damages caused by inaccuracies.

Note: Purple Toad Publishing is not advocatiing mountain climbing for children and will not assume any liability for damages.

Printing 1 2 3 4 5 6 7 8 9

Publisher's Cataloging-in-Publication Data
Leavitt, Amie Jane
Mount Fuji / Amie Jane Leavitt
p. cm.—(Man versus mountain)
Includes bibliographic references and index.
ISBN: 978-1-62469-062-4 (library bound)
1. Fuji, Mount (Japan). I. Title.
DS895.4.F85 2013
915.2—dc23
2013936508

eBook ISBN: 9781624690631

Printed by Lake Book Manufacturing, Chicago, IL

January, THURSDAY, 19. 1854.

CONTENTS

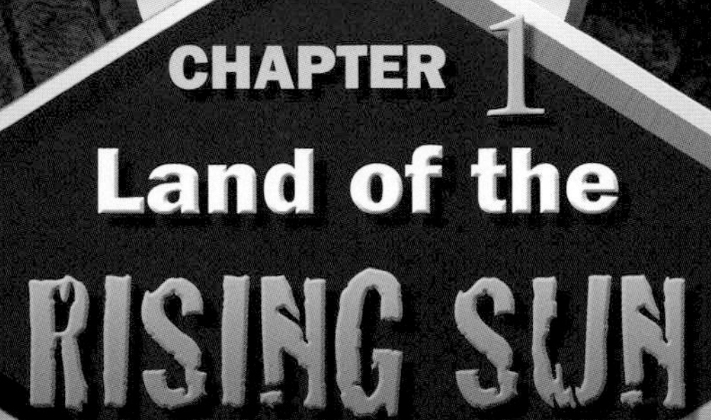

CHAPTER 1
Land of the RISING SUN

On a sunny afternoon in late July, four friends arrive at Station 5 on the Yoshidaguchi, having just taken the bus there from their apartments in downtown Tokyo. They purchase walking sticks at a souvenir shop. Even though it is hot and humid, they tie jackets around their waists and shove gloves and scarves in their backpacks. They also fill them with snacks and water, and money for the rest rooms. It will take many hours to hike to the top of Mount Fuji, and they want to be prepared. After everyone is ready to go, the friends make their way past the crowds of people to the trailhead and begin their journey to the summit.

The first part of the hike isn't hard at all. It is a smooth trail that serpentines through the forest like a long, slithering snake. Lush trees line the trail. Birds chirp, squirrels race about gathering food, and butterflies flutter from flower to flower.

Leaving Umagaeshi,
Yoshidaguchi Trail

Many Mount Fuji hikers get their walking sticks branded at each station on the way to the top. The sticks become treasured souvenirs that remind the hikers of their Fuji-san adventures.

At the sixth station, the group pays a small fee to have their walking sticks branded. They will get one of these special marks on their sticks at each of the stations. This traditional souvenir shows that they had enough courage and strength to make it all the way to the top.

Once the group passes the sixth station, the lush green vegetation has ended. There are fewer trees up here. Rough, red-black rocks cover the ground, looking much like the surface of the moon or maybe even the planet Mars. Someone reminds the hikers that these are lava rocks left over from one of Mount Fuji's many volcanic eruptions. They are like the hands of time on Mount Fuji.

The higher the group climbs, the steeper the trail becomes. Eventually, the trail does not switchback up the mountain anymore. Instead, it goes straight up. Handrails help the climbers keep their footing on the loose gravel.

At the eighth station, the friends stop for the night. They dine on small plates of curry and rice, and then slide into their sleeping bags.

They pack themselves together in the tiny hut, hoping for a few hours of sleep. It's noisy outside. Many people are still hiking on the trail. The friends all wish they had brought some earplugs to block out the sound.

Around 2:00 A.M., the group decides to start hiking again. It's too noisy to sleep, and they want to see the 4:30 sunrise from the top. Watching the sunrise from Fuji's summit is legendary. After all, Japan is the Land of the Rising Sun, and the best place to watch the sun crest the horizon in Japan is from the highest peak in the country.

At this point, the climb to the top becomes difficult. The trail becomes steeper and steeper. There are many people on the trail. They are all wearing headlamps so that they can see in the pitch-black night. In some places, there are six people, shoulder to shoulder, stretched across the trail. There is also a long line of people streaming to the top. The crowd moves at a snail's pace. Some walk a few steps and then stop to rest. Others stop alongside the trail to breathe some bottled oxygen. The air is so thin up here that, with each breath, very little oxygen reaches the lungs. The bottled oxygen helps.

At the beginning of the hike, a heavy mist had hung over the mountain. Now the clouds have lifted. The group walks up a set of stone steps past two white lion statues and underneath a *torii*. This wooden arch marks the entrance to a Shinto shrine, for many believe that Mount Fuji's summit is a holy place. Once the friends pass through the gate, they have officially made it to the top. It is very cold up there on the roof of Japan. Even though it is summertime and very warm down in Tokyo, it feels like winter on the top of Mount Fuji.

It is now within minutes of sunrise. The friends sit on some benches nd steady their cameras. The sky begins to turn from black to pale ellow, and then to dark yellow and brilliant red. The clouds begin to oil and roll as the rising sun quickly warms them. Once the fiery red n is up, the sky calms into a soft blue, and the white clouds look like ocean of frothy waves.

Ohayou gozaimasu! Good morning! A new day in Japan has just begun. Many in the group marvel at the sun rising over Mount Fuji—it is the most beautiful sight they have ever seen.

The friends take an hour to hike around the rim of its crater. The huge bowl is 820 feet (250 meters) deep,[1] about as deep as a 60-story office building is tall.

Before they leave the summit, the group eats noodles for breakfast at the highest restaurant in Japan. One person mails a letter at the post office so that it will have a cool stamp from the top of Mount Fuji. A few others get their picture taken with the big stone marker that reads (in Japanese), "This is the summit of Mount Fuji."[2] They all buy water to drink on their hike back down the mountain. There are no stations on the descent. After they get their walking sticks branded with their final Station 10 marking, they start down the steep slope to the bottom.

The sunrise on top of Mount Fuji, the roof of Japan, is a glorious sight with brilliant brushstrokes of color and dramatic movement of clouds.

A snowman points the way, but there's no mistaking that Mount Fuji towers in the distance behind him.

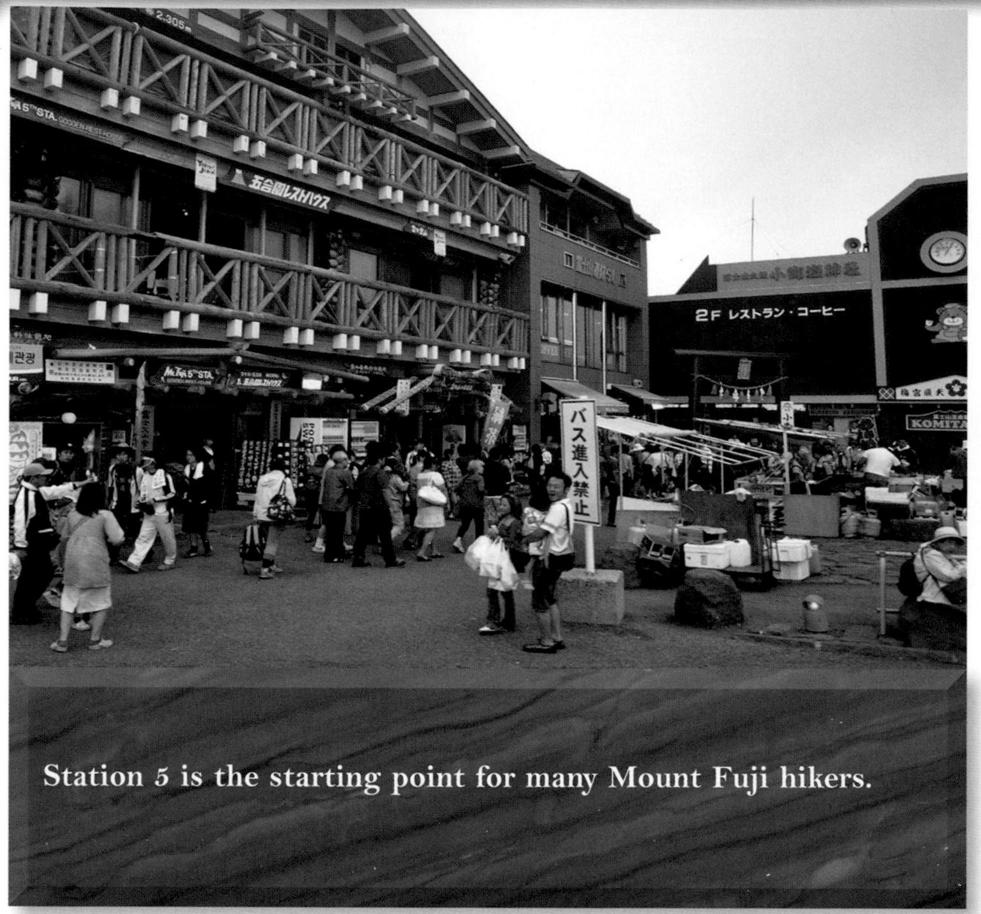

Station 5 is the starting point for many Mount Fuji hikers.

are ten stations along this trail, numbered from the bottom of the mountain to the top. Most people start their hike at Station 5, which is at about 7,562 feet (2,305 meters) of elevation. Buses from Tokyo run to this station during the official climbing season, making it extremely crowded. Some people come to Station 5 to begin their climb of Mount Fuji. Others come to be part of the excitement and watch the people who are about to embark on their journey.

At most of these stations, food and water (and restrooms) are available—for a fee. Hikers may pack supplies, but they should bring money to pay for restrooms and emergency supplies. The higher the station, the more expensive the items will be in the shops. One reason the items cost more is that they have to be carried up from Station 5 on either a person's or a pack animal's back.

Most of the stations also have souvenir shops. At Station 5, many people purchase walking sticks. Then, at each station, they can pay a small fee to have these sticks branded with a special symbol from that station. Walking sticks are very popular souvenirs from Mount Fuji. They show that a person actually climbed all the way to the top of Japan's highest peak.

Mount Fuji is a difficult hike, but it's not impossible. In fact, most people of average physical health can make it to the summit. Many children hike to the top of Mount Fuji, and some of them are accompanied by their grandparents.[3] People can usually hike to the top in five to eight hours, depending upon individual speed, the number of rests taken, and the number of people on the trail. It takes another two to three hours to hike back down. The trail down is different from the one going up. Since the trail is covered with tiny pieces of gravel and volcanic dust, most people find they do more sliding down Mount Fuji than they do hiking.

The best way to dress for a hike to the top is in layers. It may be hot at the bottom, but the top can be freezing cold. Prepared hikers wear a short-sleeve shirt and cargo pants with a lot of pockets for the lower elevations, where the temperatures are usually hot. Then, they bring other clothing in a backpack to add later, such as long underwear, sweatshirts, raincoats, long-sleeve shirts, and an extra pair of socks. In addition, many people bring scarves, gloves, sunglasses, flashlights or headlamps, a bandana, hat or cap, tissues, a towel (to wipe the sweat off their face), and a walking stick. A sturdy pair of hiking shoes is also necessary.

While on the trail, people need to be smart. The steep mountain trails change very quickly in elevation. As people move to areas of higher elevations, they can experience shortness of breath. They can also start to feel sick to their stomach or get a headache. This is called altitude sickness. To reduce the likelihood of altitude sickness, hike at a slower pace. People should stop and rest when they feel fatigued. If they start to feel ill, they should find a spot to lie down for a while.

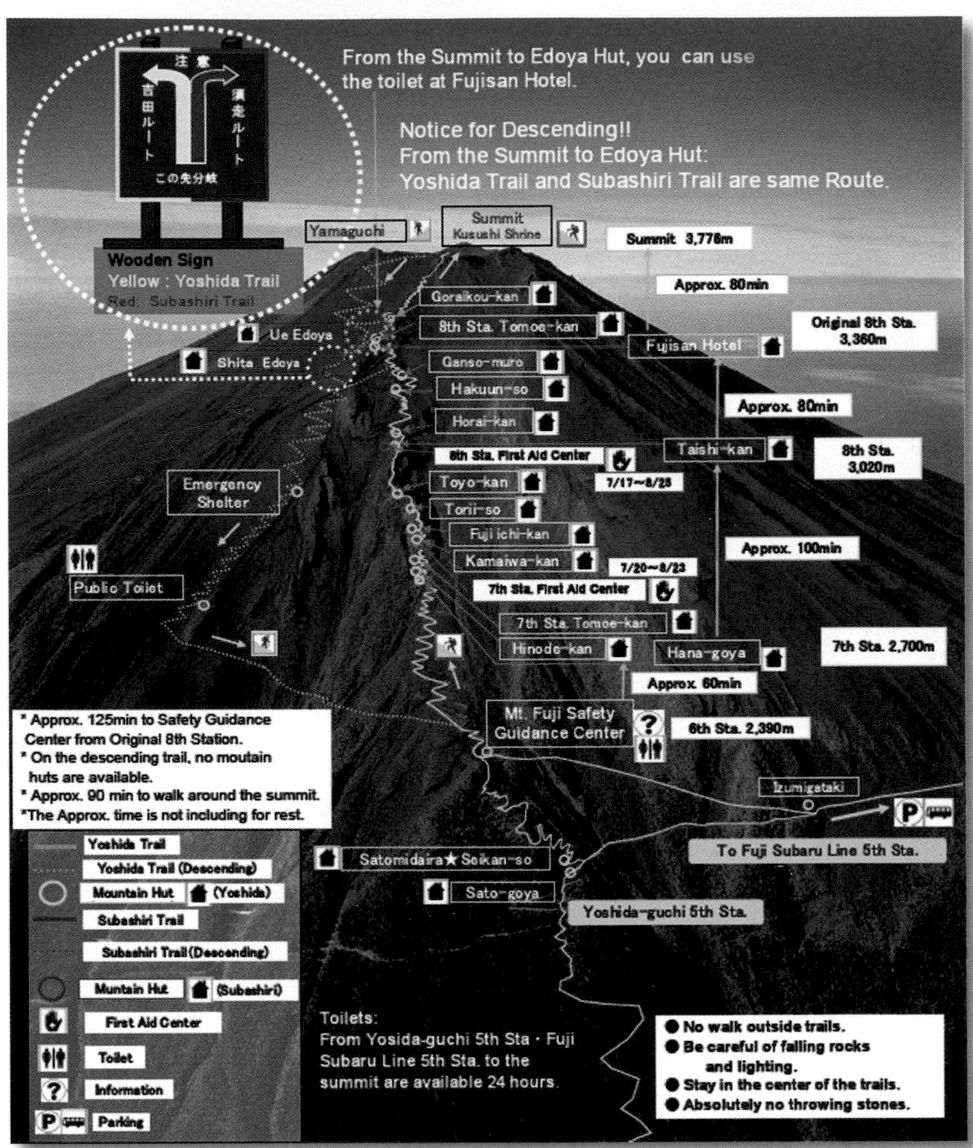

If that doesn't help, they should turn around and go partway down the mountain, then wait to climb again. The trails become more and more difficult with each foot of elevation. If a person who does not feel well continues to climb, he or she will not feel better. In fact, continuing to climb can cause serious problems later on.

Smart hikers also plan to get at least a few hours of sleep at one of the station huts. Sleeping bags and pillows are provided. All the hikers

share a room, and they are all squeezed in together. Once they spend hours climbing the mountain, they hardly care about the tight space and are just grateful for a place to rest their exhausted bodies. Hikers must reserve their spots in the huts in advance. There are only a few spots available in comparison to the large number of people on the trails.

Hikers must always take out what they bring in. Hundreds of thousands of people visit Mount Fuji every year. If everyone tossed their trash to the side of the path, the mountain would look like a giant landfill. Despite the rule, some people have been inconsiderate and left their garbage on the trails. This has had a negative impact on the mountain. For years, the government has been asking the United Nations Educational, Scientific, and Cultural Organization (UNESCO) to declare Mount Fuji a World Heritage Site. This distinction would bring

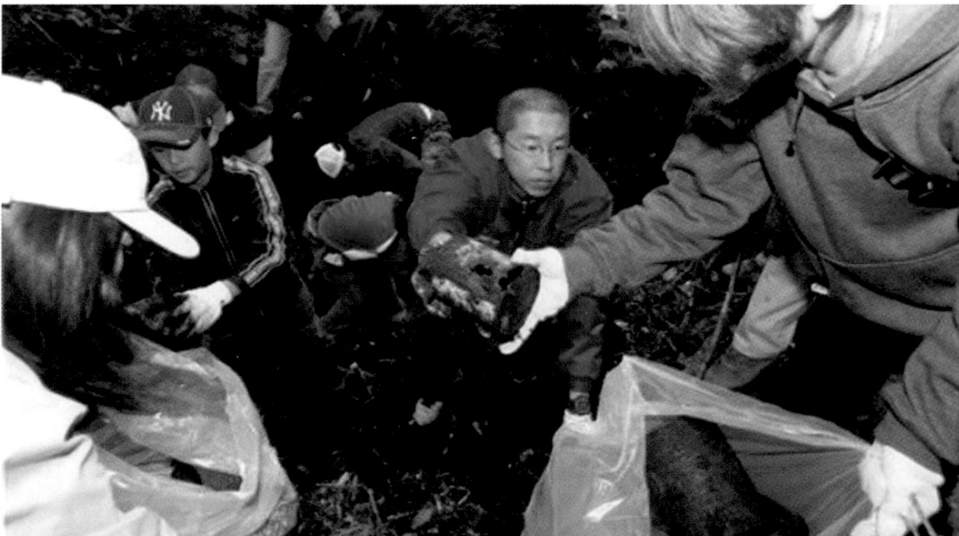

Sadly, people throw garbage onto the trails of Mount Fuji. Fortunately, people concerned with the environment are making an effort to protect the sacred mountain. They work together as families, friends, coworkers, and activists to clean the mess and keep Mount Fuji a beautiful place to visit.

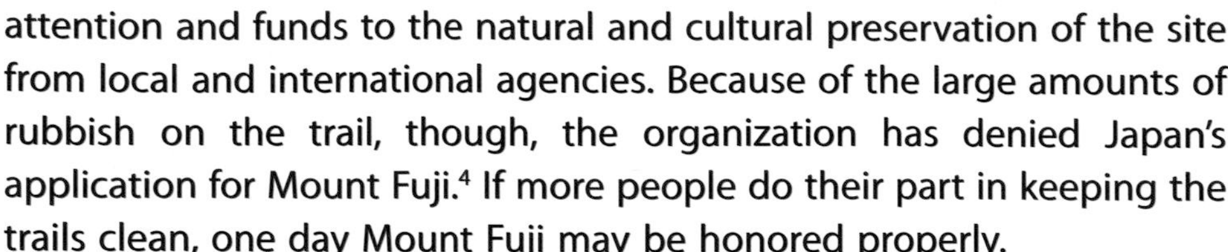

attention and funds to the natural and cultural preservation of the site from local and international agencies. Because of the large amounts of rubbish on the trail, though, the organization has denied Japan's application for Mount Fuji.[4] If more people do their part in keeping the trails clean, one day Mount Fuji may be honored properly.

Along the trails of Mount Fuji are several wooden archways. These gates, called *toriis*, mark the entrance to sacred Shinto shrines. The Japanese people have always considered Mount Fuji to be a sacred place. In days of old, pilgrims climbed the mountain in order to have a spiritual experience. If hikers can think of the beauty of the mountain as they pass through the *toriis*, maybe they will be moved to leave Mount Fuji better than they found it.

Along with *toriis*, there are also shrines and Buddhist temples. At the summit, there is a shrine to the deity of Mount Fuji. She is the Shinto deity Princess Konohanasakuya. It is believed that she rode a white horse to the top of Mount Fuji and then ascended into Heaven. The shrine marks the spot where Shinto followers believe the princess left this earth.[5]

The Fujiyoshida Sengen shrine dates back to 1615.

Running to the Summit

Some runners like to push the limit. They want to test their endurance in some of the most extreme places on Earth. Some dash across 150 miles (240 kilometers) of the Sahara's scorching sands. Others scurry along Antarctica's icy trails. And still others race up steep gravel trails to the summit of Mount Fuji.

The first Fuji Mountain Race was held in 1947. Every year since, the race has attracted thousands of competitors. In order to run in the race, people must qualify for it. They have to prove that they have completed other races in certain amounts of time.

Runners must finish the 13-mile (21-kilometer) Fuji Mountain Race in 4½ hours or less. In order to do this, they have to be moving along the trail at a fairly brisk pace. It's hard enough to climb Mount Fuji at a turtle's pace, let alone run all the way to the top like a gazelle. About half the people who enter the race are unable to finish it.[6] This race undoubtedly tests one's endurance.

Fuji Mountain Race

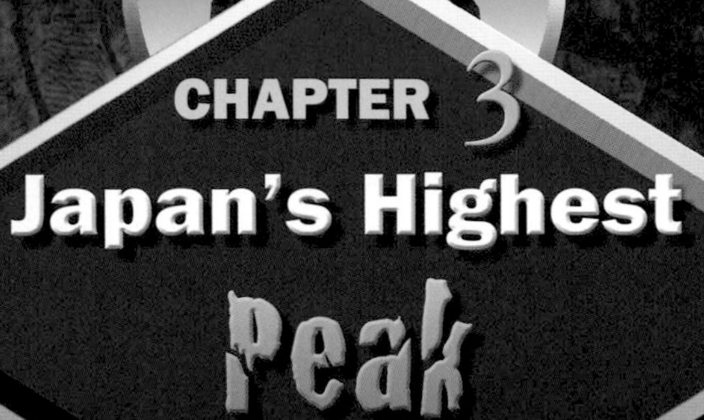

CHAPTER 3
Japan's Highest Peak

Mount Fuji is in the country of Japan. This island nation is surrounded by the Pacific Ocean and, to the west, the Sea of Japan. It is part of Asia.

Japan has four main islands and more than 4,000 smaller islands. It is just a bit smaller than the state of California.[1] Mount Fuji, Japan's highest peak, is on Honshu, its largest island. This island is also where the capital city of Tokyo is located. In fact, Tokyo is only about 70 miles (112 kilometers) from Mount Fuji—less than a two-hour drive. With nearly 9 million people living in and around Tokyo, it is one of the most populated cities in Japan.

Japan lies along the Ring of Fire—a volatile region around the Pacific Ocean. The Ring of Fire is the result of how the earth is put together.

The earth is made of different layers. The center part is called the core, just like the seedy center of an apple. The core has two areas—the inner core and the outer

Fuji on beautiful
Honshu Island

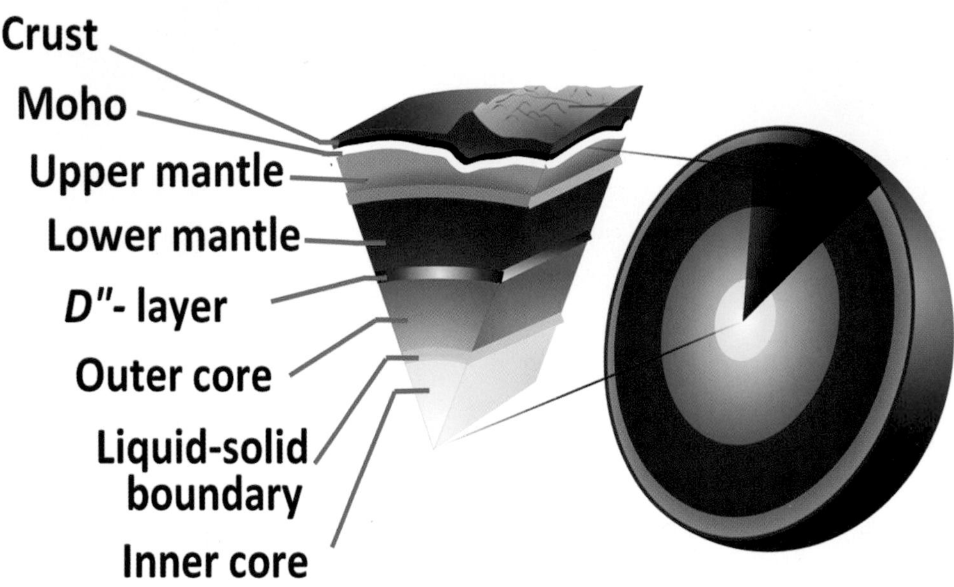

There is hot magma (liquid rock) in Earth's mantle. This magma pushes its way through Earth's crust and forms volcanoes like Mount Fuji.

core. The inner core is made of solid iron. The outer core is made up of molten iron mixed with sulfur.

Surrounding the core is the mantle. This layer contains liquid rock, called magma. The mantle makes up 84 percent of the earth,[2] so it is the largest section of the earth's interior.

The thin outer layer is called the crust, like the crust on a loaf of bread. Earth's crust is not one solid piece, though. Each enormous piece is called a tectonic plate. The areas where the plates meet are called plate boundaries. The plates float on the mantle, slowly sliding toward or away from one another. A convergent plate boundary is where plates push against one another. They can violently crash, causing the earth to quake and mountains to form. They can gradually push one another up, making mountains taller. A divergent plate boundary is where the plates pull apart. Magma from the mantle can rush up through the opening, causing volcanic eruptions. Earthquakes and

eruptions can happen at other places on earth, but there is definitely more of this activity at plate boundaries than elsewhere.

The Ring of Fire makes a horseshoe around the Pacific plate boundary. In some areas, the Pacific plate converges with a neighboring plate. In other areas, it diverges from a neighboring plate. All that movement causes a lot of stress along the plate boundaries, making earthquakes and volcanoes common there. In fact, the volcanoes are what give this region its fiery name. There are more volcanoes along the Ring of Fire than anywhere else on Earth. It has 452 known volcanoes, or 90 percent of all the volcanoes on earth.[3] They include Mount St. Helens and Mount Rainier in Washington State, Krakatoa in Indonesia, Mount Ruapehu in New Zealand, and Mount Fuji in Japan.

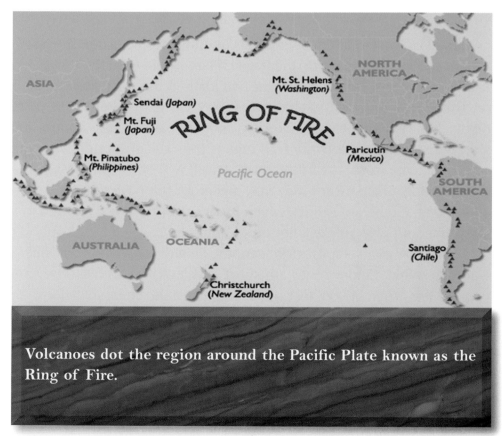

Volcanoes dot the region around the Pacific Plate known as the Ring of Fire.

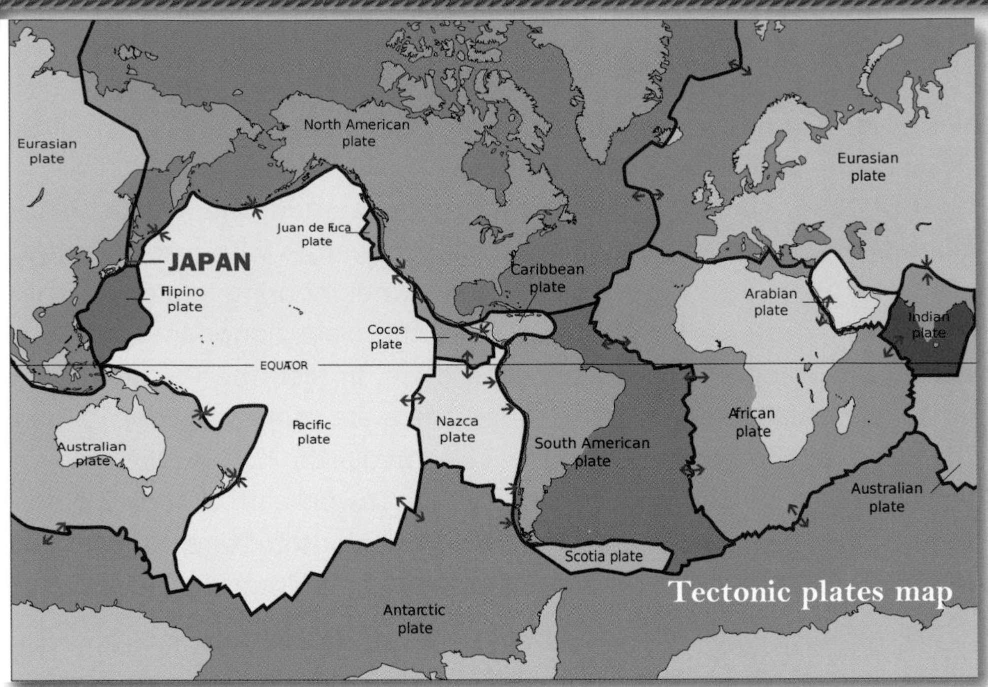

Tectonic plates map

Japan is situated at the boundaries of four tectonic plates: the North American Plate in the north, the Pacific Plate in the east, the Philippine Sea Plate in the south, and the Eurasian Plate in the west. Mount Fuji is on the North American plate and is very close to where that plate meets the Philippine and Eurasian plates.[4] Japan has about 200 volcanoes. Some are active, which means they still erupt or have some type of activity (such as earth tremors, lava flows, or ash plumes). Some are dormant, which means they may still erupt but have not done so in a long time. Some are extinct, which means they have not erupted in a long time and probably will not erupt again.

There are many types of volcanoes. Shield volcanoes look like a warrior's shield. Cinder cones are short and look like anthills. They are usually less than 1,000 feet (300 meters) tall. Stratovolcanoes, or composite volcanoes, are shaped like the cinder cones, but they are much larger. They continue to grow taller with each eruption. Over time, they can reach 10,000 feet (3,000 meters) or more.[5] There are many stratovolcanoes along the Ring of Fire, including Mount Fuji, Mount Rainier, Mount St. Helens, Krakatoa, and Mount Ruapehu.

Mount Fuji is a nearly symmetrical stratovolcano. It looks the same on both sides. Its top has been sliced off in an even horizontal line, almost as if it were cut off with a sharp knife.

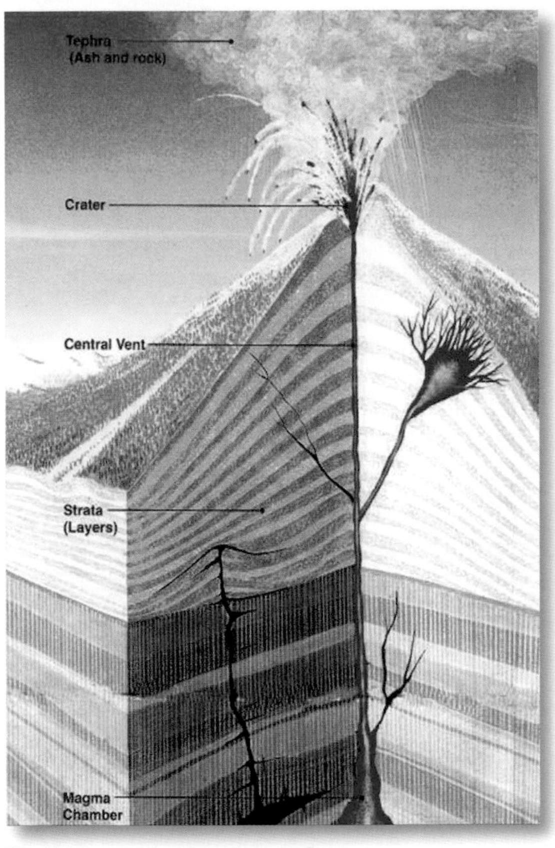

Boiling magma is under great pressure. It pushes its way out of Earth's crust in what is known as a volcanic eruption.

Like other stratovolcanoes, Mount Fuji has a central vent. It leads from the magma chamber beneath the tectonic plate all the way to the top of the volcano like a long straw. This vent allows lava to flow up from the mantle. As magma continues to push its way into the vent, the pressure inside the tube increases. It's kind of like when a person shakes a can of soda—the pressure inside the can builds and builds until finally, when the top is opened, the soda sprays everywhere. This is what happens inside the vent of a stratovolcano. The magma keeps pushing its way inside from the magma chamber, the pressure inside the vent keeps building, until suddenly *BOOM,* the magma explodes through the vent's opening, along with dust, ash, rocks, and mud. Sometimes the magma does not reach the main vent opening at the top. Instead, it will erupt from the side of the volcano.[6]

Although Mount Fuji has erupted more than 2,200 times over its lifetime, it hasn't erupted since 1707. Since three hundred years have

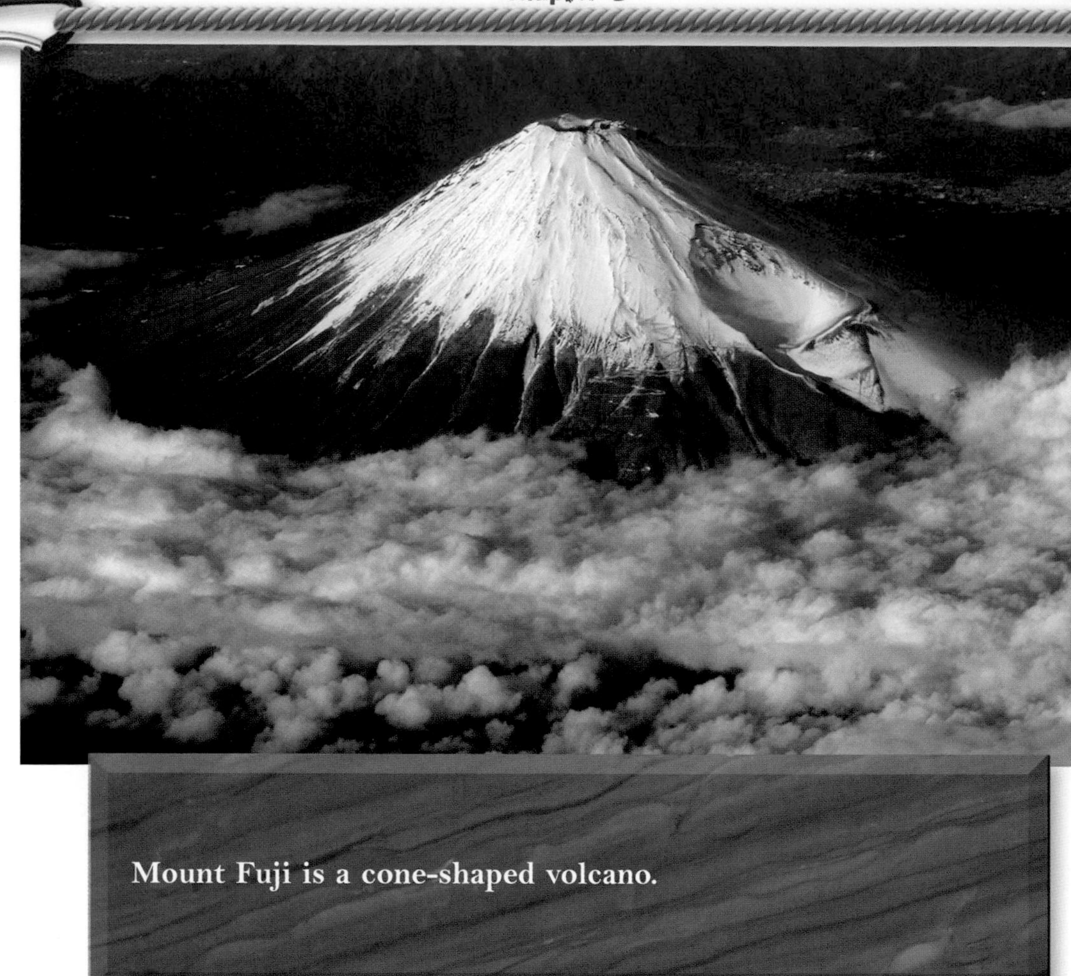

Mount Fuji is a cone-shaped volcano.

gone by, Mount Fuji is often called extinct. It is not. Mount Fuji is still active. It has shown signs of unrest, especially since the year 2000. In 2000 and 2001, scientists recorded a series of earthquakes under the volcano. In 2011, a major earthquake near Japan added more pressure to Mount Fuji's chamber. Steam and other hot gases often billow from the crater, and water sprays from vents nearby. The pressure inside the volcano is also greater than it was before its last major eruption in 1707. These are all warning signs that the volcano will erupt again. In May 2012, a scientist at Ryukyu University predicted that Mount Fuji could erupt within the next several years.[7]

It's Going to Blow!

It's not a matter of *if* Mount Fuji will erupt, but a matter of *when.* Scientists are very concerned about this eruption and what will happen to the millions of people who live nearby. Mount Fuji's last eruption in 1707 covered Tokyo in several inches of ash. It was followed by a powerful 8.4-magnitude earthquake.[8] The disaster killed approximately 20,000 people.[9] Scientists want to do everything possible to prevent a similar tragedy. They can't stop the volcano from erupting, but they can help people prepare. They are encouraging the Japanese government and the people who live in the area to develop emergency plans.

First, the country needs to decide how it will warn people and move them out of the path of danger. The government should also have food, water, and medicine ready for people who might need it. They should have these supplies in various places throughout the country so that they can be accessed quickly and easily. More people should be trained in firefighting and emergency medical care to help those in need.[10]

The city of Fujiyoshida, a town very close to Mount Fuji, suggests plans for individuals. They recommend stashing a backpack with emergency supplies and food for each person in each family. That way, everyone can quickly grab what they need when the city is evacuated.[11] Some things to include in an emergency backpack are

- first-aid kit
- water
- nonperishable food
- flashlights with extra batteries
- blankets
- clothes

. period drawing of Mount Fuji's
ıst eruption

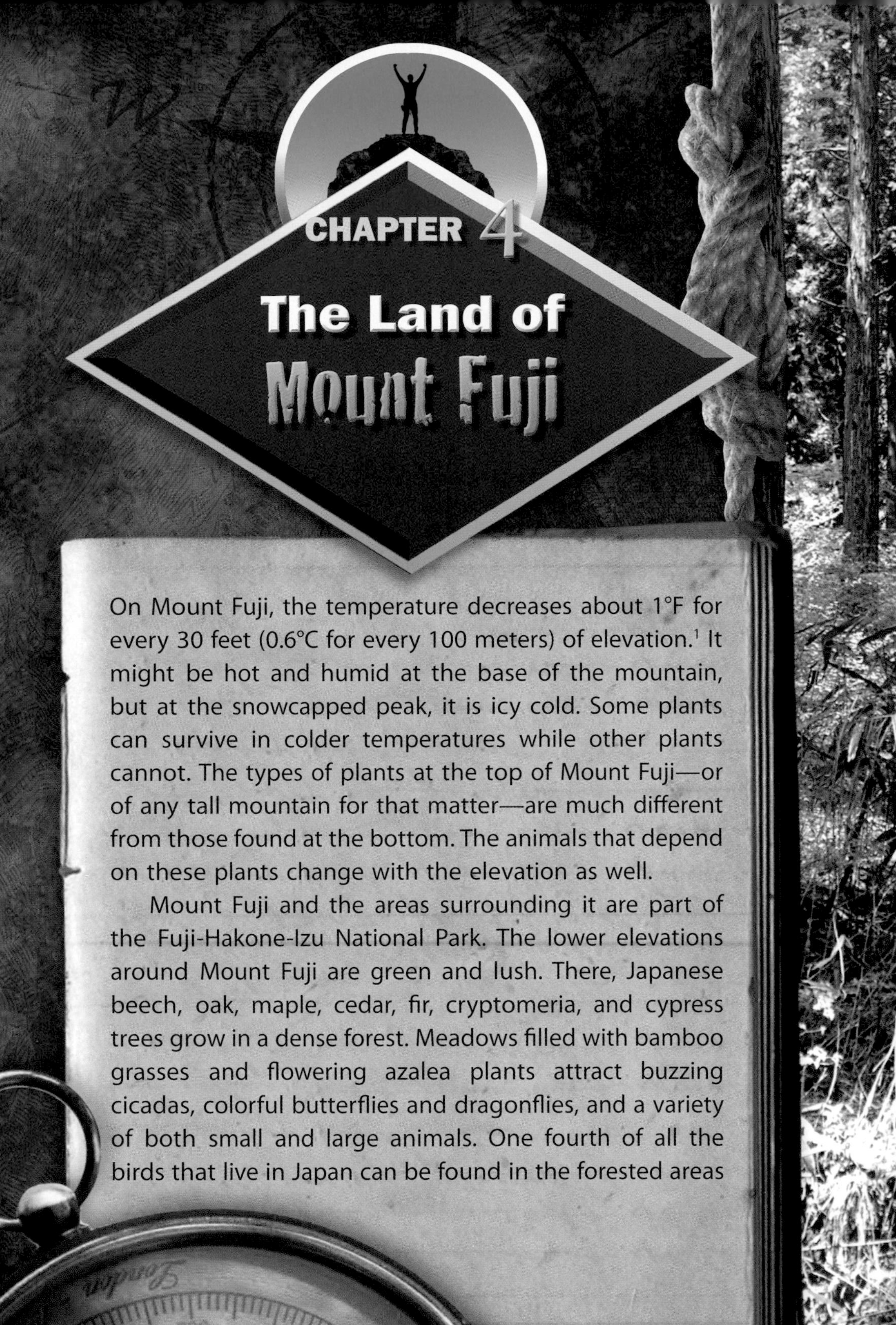

CHAPTER 4
The Land of Mount Fuji

On Mount Fuji, the temperature decreases about 1°F for every 30 feet (0.6°C for every 100 meters) of elevation.[1] It might be hot and humid at the base of the mountain, but at the snowcapped peak, it is icy cold. Some plants can survive in colder temperatures while other plants cannot. The types of plants at the top of Mount Fuji—or of any tall mountain for that matter—are much different from those found at the bottom. The animals that depend on these plants change with the elevation as well.

Mount Fuji and the areas surrounding it are part of the Fuji-Hakone-Izu National Park. The lower elevations around Mount Fuji are green and lush. There, Japanese beech, oak, maple, cedar, fir, cryptomeria, and cypress trees grow in a dense forest. Meadows filled with bamboo grasses and flowering azalea plants attract buzzing cicadas, colorful butterflies and dragonflies, and a variety of both small and large animals. One fourth of all the birds that live in Japan can be found in the forested areas

Fuji-Hakone-Izu
National Park

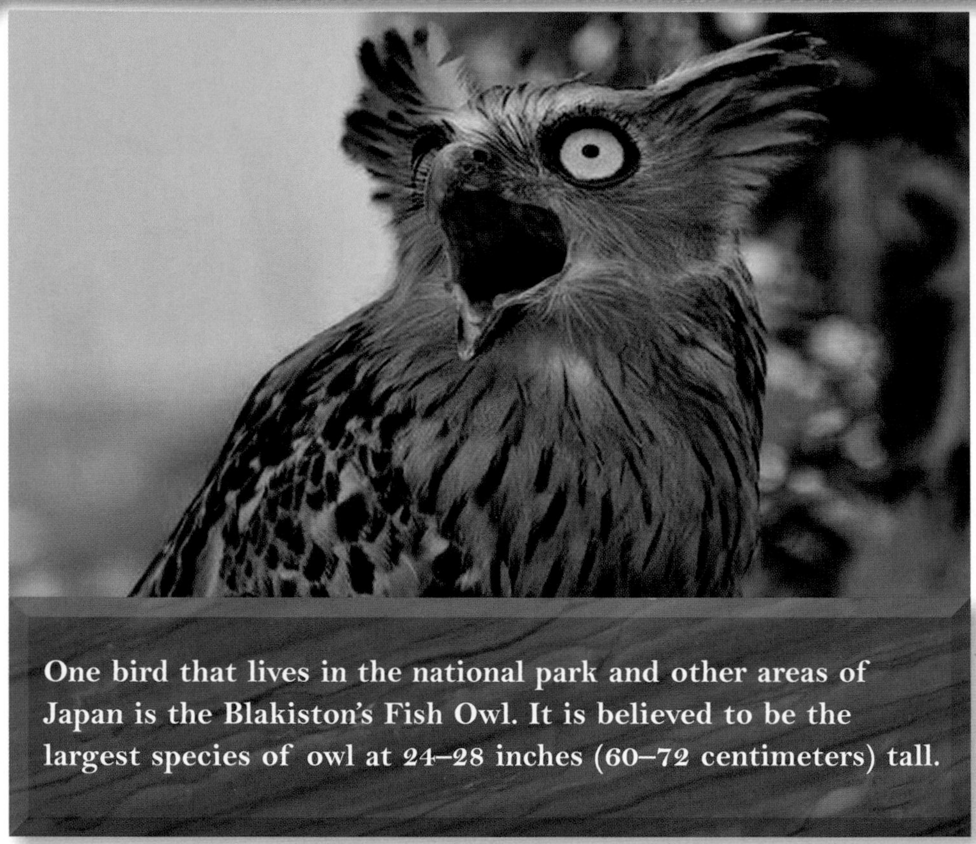

One bird that lives in the national park and other areas of Japan is the Blakiston's Fish Owl. It is believed to be the largest species of owl at 24–28 inches (60–72 centimeters) tall.

at the base of Mount Fuji.[2] That's about 180 species.[3] There are flycatchers, warblers, owls, nutcrackers, thrushes, and many, many others.

Higher up, the vegetation decreases. The trees are shorter. The plants are sparser. Eventually, above the treeline, no trees grow at all. In this area, grasses, small shrubs, mosses, and other tiny plants grow.

Mammals are plentiful on Mount Fuji at the various elevations. Among the 40 different species of mammals are the Japanese squirrel and the Japanese dormouse. Larger mammals such as the Asian black bear and the Japanese serow (a goat-like animal) are also found in the forest and at higher elevations.[4]

Fuji is known for its sparkling clean natural springs with pure, clear water. The water comes from the approximately 2.2 billion tons of rain and snow that fall on Mount Fuji every year.[5] To put this in perspective,

this is equivalent in volume to the water in 880 Olympic-size swimming pools![6] This water seeps down into the earth and forms underground streams and rivers. It provides clean drinking water for people in the surrounding area.

Water-related attractions bring visitors to Fuji-Hakone-Izu National Park every year. Natural hot springs are big pools of warm water, like large hot tubs formed by nature. Areas with volcanic activity often have hot springs. The magma that flows beneath the earth's surface heats the nearby groundwater. When this heated groundwater reaches the surface, it collects in pools called hot springs. Hakone is a popular hot spring resort located at the northern base of Mount Fuji.

The Five Lakes region is another popular recreation site. The lakes, also at the northern base of Mount Fuji, were formed when lava dammed up the rivers in the area. Three of the lakes are connected through underground waterways, so their water level remains the same all the time. When the level in one lake changes, it does in the other two as well. Every year, thousands of people escape the crowded conditions of Tokyo to enjoy nature in the Five Lakes region. They boat, fish, wind surf, have picnics by the shore, camp in one of the many campgrounds, or relax in a comfortable hotel. Mount Fuji can be seen from all of the lakes, yet two of them—Lake Motosuko and Lake Yamanakako—have the best views of the sacred mountain.

Many cities, towns, and villages are located in the Mount Fuji area. Fujiyoshida, the largest city in this area, is on the northern slopes of the Five Lakes region. It is about a two-hour bus or car ride from Tokyo, which is located to the northeast. Fujiyoshida was a historic starting point for pilgrimages to Mount Fuji's summit. Hikers would start at the Fuji Sengen Shrine. There, they would pray for a safe journey. This shrine was built and dedicated to Mount Fuji in 788 CE. Many people still visit the shrine before they begin their Mount Fuji hike.

Fujiyoshida is also the home of one of the world's fastest roller coasters, which is at the Fuji-Q High Land amusement park.[7] This city has a modern economy that focuses on trade, tourism, and technology.

Fuji-Q High Land roller coaster

In earlier years, people tried to farm the area, but they found it was too difficult to grow crops successfully on the rugged lava fields. They started home businesses of weaving. Soon the area became known for its textiles. Textile manufacturing is still important around Fuji.[8]

Kanagawa, which is northeast of Mount Fuji, includes the hot springs of Hakone. It was from this view of Mount Fuji that revered Japanese artist Katsushika Hokusai designed his most famous woodcut print, *The Great Wave off Kanagawa,* in the early 1830s. This piece of artwork features Mount Fuji in the background. Kanagawa today includes the busy coastal port city of Yokohama and smaller mountain villages.

Fujinomiya is on the lower slopes of Mount Fuji's southeastern side. The city has been around since ancient days. It was originally a post town, which means merchants and travelers could stop there to eat and rest. Now it is an industrial center with many papermaking factories. Fujinomiya is also a starting point for a hike up Mount Fuji. From there, the same trail is used for going up and for coming down. This is the preferred trail for people coming from the east side of the island.

At the base of Mount Fuji, a pale blue butterfly flutters in a sea of lime-green grasslands. It stops to drink the nectar of flowers and lays tiny eggs on the underside of shrub leaves. This is the endangered Reverdin's Blue butterfly. Its habitat is shrinking every year. In some places of Japan, this butterfly is already extinct.[9] The Nashigahara grasslands is one of the few remaining places that the butterfly still lives in Japan.

Scientists and volunteers with Earthwatch Institute go to the Nashigahara grasslands to study the butterfly. Most of them are from Japan, but some come from other countries as well, including Australia and the United States. They watch how and where the insect lays its eggs. They watch to see what kinds of flowers it depends on for food. They observe where the caterpillars hang in their chrysalis stage while they turn into butterflies. They see which animals are natural predators of the butterfly.[10] These efforts are helping scientists learn more about this insect so that they can help protect it and prevent it from becoming extinct.

In their research, the scientists have learned that the Reverdin's Blue lays its eggs on and feeds on only one particular plant, a shrub called *Indigofera*. The Reverdin's Blue also has a bodyguard, a certain species of ant. This ant protects the butterflies' eggs from being eaten by other animals.[11]

The Reverdin's Blue butterfly

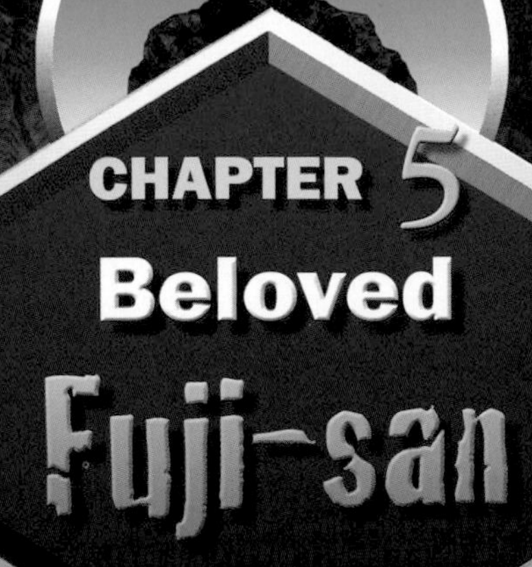

CHAPTER 5
Beloved Fuji-san

A month after their first hike on the Yoshidaguchi Trail, the same group of friends from Tokyo has returned to the mountain. This time they are staying in the town of Fujiyoshida. They have not come to hike the mountain again but rather to celebrate the close of the hiking season in the grand Fire Festival, or Yoshida no Himatsuri.

At two o'clock on August 26, the friends enter the Fuji Sengen Shrine. At this sacred place, they learn that the Fire Festival has been a tradition on the northern slopes of Mount Fuji for more than 500 years. The festival is held to appease the goddess of Mount Fuji and convince the volcano not to erupt again for another year.

It is here at the shrine that the goddess's soul is believed to dwell. For the festival, her soul is carried in a portable shrine called an *omikoshi*. The friends watch as thirty strong men lift the *omikoshi*. The shrine must be very heavy, because the men struggle to hoist it onto

The Fire Festival

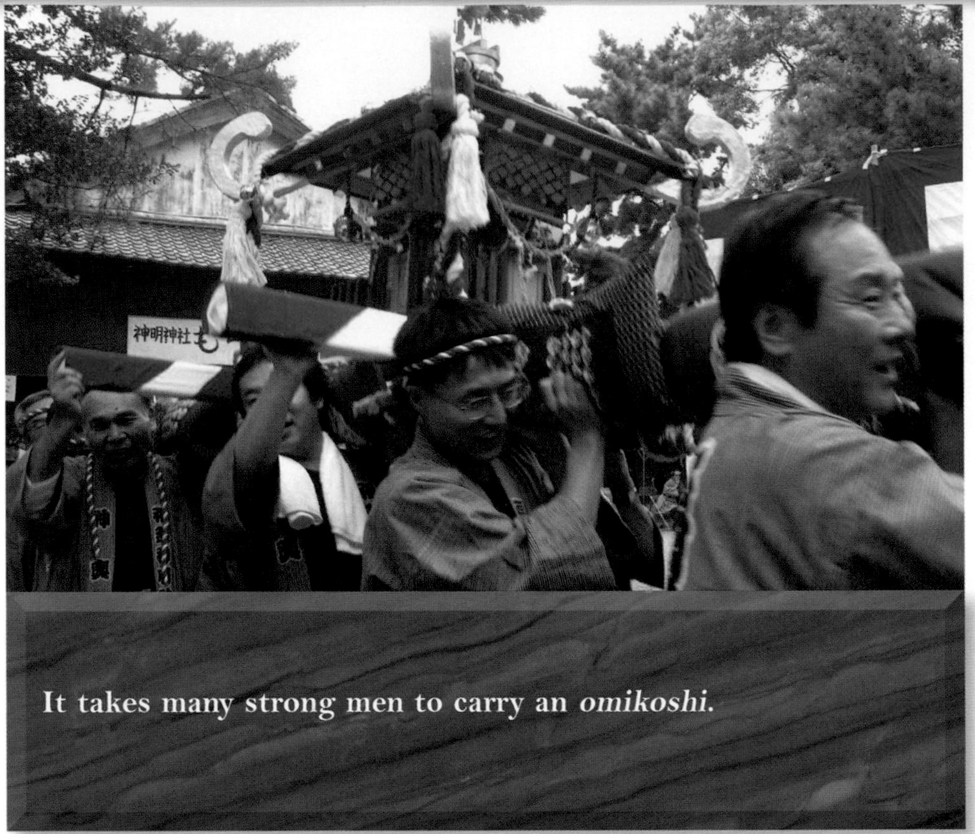

It takes many strong men to carry an *omikoshi*.

their shoulders. Someone next to the group tells the friends that the shrine weighs more than two thousand pounds (one metric ton).

Once the men have the shrine on their shoulders, they prepare to leave Fuji Sengen. They are going to parade the goddess through the city. They want to show her the value of the city so that she can understand why she should protect it from a volcanic eruption.

The *omikoshi* is called the myojin mikoshi. It is not the only shrine to be paraded through the city this day. The mikage mikoshi follows the myojin. It is a giant version of Mount Fuji, painted tangerine orange.

The friends leave the shrine and race to a spot on the street to watch the grand parade. As the men pass with the shrines, torches and bonfires are lit down the middle of the street. These fires represent the exploding flames of a volcanic eruption and are meant to impress the goddess. They hope she will be convinced that these tamed flames are much better than any lava eruption that could come from the crater of Mount Fuji.

It seems that everyone in the city and surrounding countryside has come to the festival. The crowded streets burst with energy. It is one of the most exciting times of the year to be in Fujiyoshida.

Mount Fuji has been an important part of Japanese culture since Japan's first inhabitants settled on its islands. The mountain has been central to the country's culture, legends, religion, and artwork for centuries. The Yoshida no Himatsuri is just one of many examples of how Mount Fuji remains an essential part of the Japanese way of life.

Japanese legends about Mount Fuji are many. There are some about how the mountain was formed. There are some about how and why it erupts. Many of these legends show the Japanese people's deep connection to nature. The Shinto religion—which originated in Japan—teaches that all of nature must be respected. It also teaches that certain important landforms in nature are deities and should be both treasured and worshiped. The Japanese people hold Mount Fuji close to their hearts.

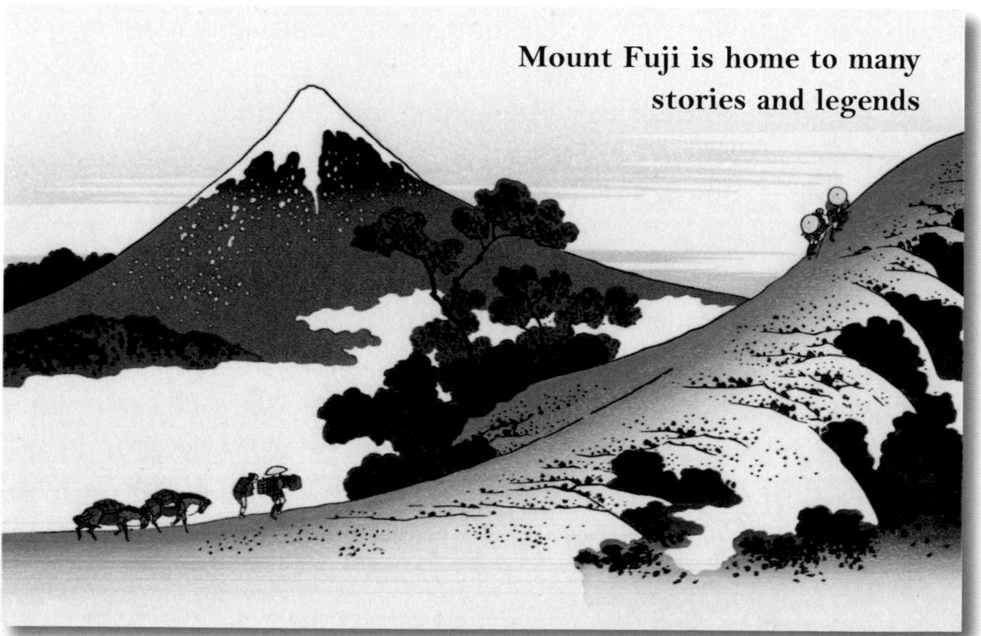

Mount Fuji is home to many stories and legends

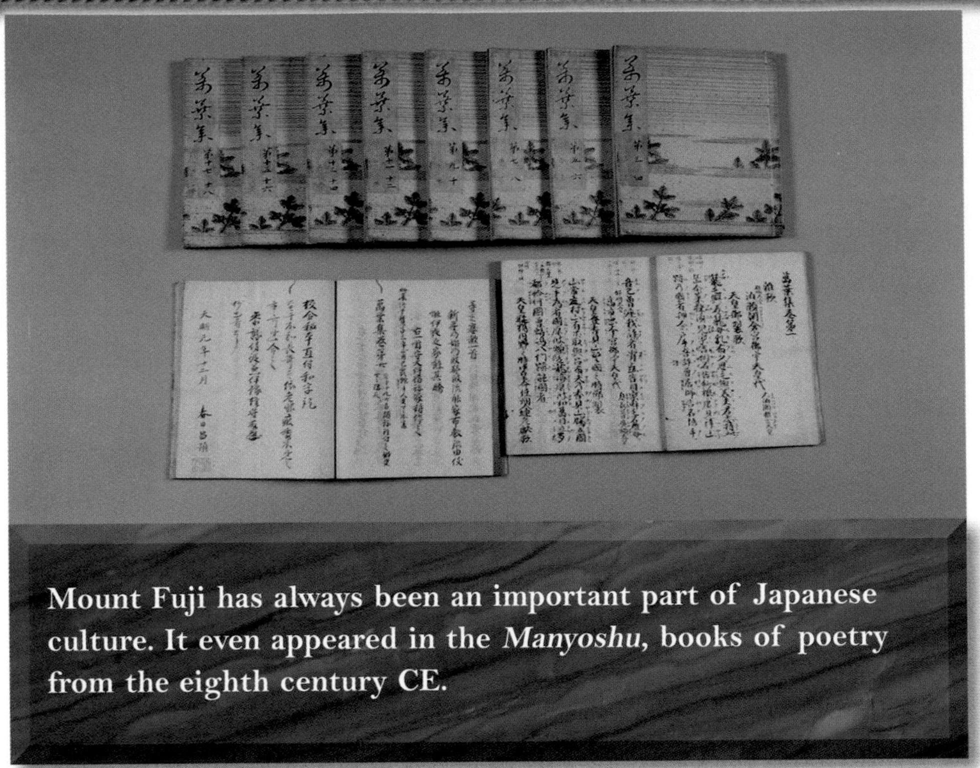

Mount Fuji has always been an important part of Japanese culture. It even appeared in the *Manyoshu*, books of poetry from the eighth century CE.

Mount Fuji has also been important in Japanese literature. It is mentioned in the oldest books of Japanese poetry, called the *Manyoshu*, which were compiled in 759 CE. One passage, translated, reads:

> Passing through Tago Bay and coming to a clearing,
> I see snow falling,
> pure white,
> on Fuji's lofty peak.[1]

The mountain is also mentioned in Japan's oldest stories, including *The Tale of the Bamboo Cutter*, which was written in 1,000 CE, and is depicted in Japanese artwork. One of the most famous artists to include Mount Fuji in his work is Katsushika Hokusai. He lived in Japan in the early 1800s. He was a woodcut-print artist who created the *Thirty-six Views of Mount Fuji*. These prints became famous all over the world, especially his *The Great Wave off Kanagawa* and *Red Fuji*. Hokusai's

prints have remained popular for nearly 200 years. Many Japanese artists continue to include the image of Mount Fuji in their work.

For centuries, Mount Fuji has been a popular image for Japanese people to use in their home décor. Many hang pictures of Mount Fuji in their homes because it is a symbol of good luck. They sometimes build miniature versions of Mount Fuji in their gardens.

There are two symbols in Japan that are most revered. The first is the nation's flag, which is plain white with a brilliant red circle in the middle. This flag represents Japan as the Land of the Rising Sun. The second symbol is Mount Fuji. It represents strength, perseverance, and a history of spirituality among the people. One Japanese person explained to a *National Geographic* reporter in 2002, "Japan without Fuji, would be like America without the Statue of Liberty."[2]

Fuji-san is beloved by the people and immensely important to the country and its culture. It has been that way for centuries.

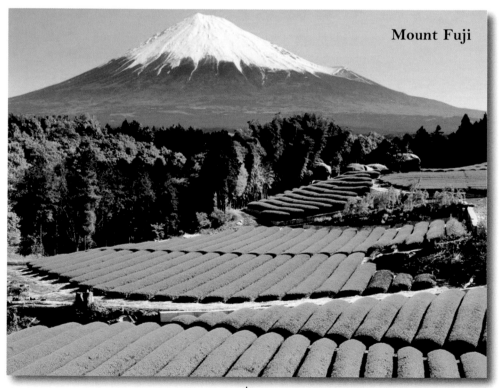

Mount Fuji

The Legend of Fuji-Yama

Legend has it that the first person to see Mount Fuji was a man who lived in the woods. His name was Visu. One night, Visu and his entire family were asleep in bed. Suddenly, the earth roared and rumbled as it quaked tremendously. Everyone in the house leaped from their beds and ran to the door to find safety outside. When they opened the cabin door, they were greeted by an unusual sight. The earth around them had changed dramatically. Where there used to be flat land, an enormously tall mountain now stood. It was a perfect cone shape and covered in a blanket of snow. Visu felt that this mountain was special above all others and named it Fuji-Yama, the everlasting mountain.[3]

A shooting star falls over Mount Fuji at dusk.

How Does Fuji Compare?

Just how tall is Mount Fuji in comparison to other sites on Earth? Here are some figures to help put it into perspective.

- Mount Everest is the tallest mountain in the world. It stands 29,029 feet (8,848 meters) high. It would take more than two of Mount Fuji to reach the top of Mount Everest.
- Burj Khalifa is the tallest building in the world. It would take 4½ Burj Khalifa buildings stacked on top of one another to reach the top of Mount Fuji.
- The Empire State Building in New York was once the tallest building in the world. It would take 8½ Empire State Buildings to reach the top of Mount Fuji.
- Big Ben is a famous clock tower in London. It would take 39 Big Ben clock towers to reach the top of Mount Fuji.

Big Ben is located in London, England, by the Parliament Building on the Thames River.

Chapter One: Land of the Rising Sun

1. Nasa Earth Observatory, Mount Fuji, http://earthobservatory.nasa.gov/IOTD/view.php?id=4286
2. "Mt. Fuji Climb: Yoshida Trail from Kawaguchiko," *Tokyo Times,* July 7, 2010, http://www.tokyotimes.com/post/en/1191/Mt+Fuji+Climb+Yoshida+Trail+from+Kawaguchiko.html
3. Tracy Dahlby, "Mount Fuji: An Iconic Peak—and Trek," Cnn.com, *Budget Travel Online,* March 30, 2007, http://www.cnn.com/2007/TRAVEL/DESTINATIONS/03/30/mt.fuji/index.html
4. Tracy Dahlby, "Fuji," *National Geographic,* August 2002, p. 26.
5. "Discover Japan: Mount Fuji—A Spiritual and Cultural Symbol," http://www.hiraganatimes.com/hp/travel/discover/kiji262e.html
6. Ronald E. Yates, "Mt. Fuji Climbers Find Its Grandeur Slipping," *Chicago Tribune,* March 24, 1986, http://articles.chicagotribune.com/1986-03-24/news/8601210974_1_fuji-volcanic-ash-mt
7. "The Tragic Tale of Sir Rutherford Alcock's Dog," http://www.takaoclub.com/alcock/index.htm

Chapter Two: Climbing to the Top

1. Welcome to Japan: National Parks, Fuji-Hakone-Izu National Park, http://www.welcome-to.jp/nationalparks/Fuji.html
2. "Volcano Myths and Legends—Japan," Oregon State University, http://volcano.oregonstate.edu/oldroot/legends/japan/japan.html
3. "Mount Fuji," Frommer's, http://www.frommers.com/destinations/tokyo/0085020381.html
4. Tracy Dahlby, "Fuji," *National Geographic,* August 2002, p. 26.
5. Shizuoka Prefecture: Mount Fuji Trivial Fact Quiz, "The Diety of Mount Fuji," http://www.pref.shizuoka.jp/a_foreign/english/fujiquiz/answer02.html
6. Fuji Mountain Race, Fujiyoshida City Official Web Site, http://www.city.fujiyoshida.yamanashi.jp/div/english/html/race.html

Chapter Three: Japan's Highest Peak

1. *CIA World Factbook,* Japan, https://www.cia.gov/library/publications/the-world-factbook/geos/ja.html
2. National Museum of Natural History: "The Dynamic Earth," http://www.mnh.si.edu/earth/text/4_1_4_0.html
3. National Geographic, "Volcanoes, Earth's Fiery Power," http://environment.nationalgeographic.com/environment/natural-disasters/volcano-profile/
4. "Plate Tectonics: Faulty Thinking." *The Economist,* March 17, 2011, http://www.economist.com/node/18398762
5. Pacific Disaster Center, Volcano, http://www.pdc.org/iweb/volcano.jsp?subg=1
6. Mount Fuji Volcanic Hazard Map, http://www.city.fujiyoshida.yamanashi.jp/div/bosai/html/hazard_map/q_and_a.html

7. Clark Liat, "Pressure in Mount Fuji Is Now Higher than Last Eruption, Warn Experts," *Wired.co.uk,* September 6, 2012, http://www.wired.co.uk/news/archive/2012-09/06/mount-fuji
8. Tracy Dahlby, "Fuji," *National Geographic,* August 2002, p. 26.
9. "Experts Discuss Evacuation Plan in the Event of Mt. Fuji Eruption," *Japan Today,* June 10, 2012, http://www.japantoday.com/category/national/view/experts-discuss-evacuation-plan-in-the-event-of-mt-fuji-eruption
10. "What Can Be Done to Mitigate the Effects of a Looming Mt. Fuji Eruption?" Forbes.com, September 11, 2012, http://www.forbes.com/sites/quora/2012/09/11/what-can-be-done-to-mitigate-the-effects-of-the-looming-mt-fuji-eruption/
11. Mount Fuji Volcanic Hazard Map, http://www.city.fujiyoshida.yamanashi.jp/div/bosai/html/hazard_map/q_and_a.html

Chapter Four: The Land of Mount Fuji

1. Fujisan.net, Mt Fuji's Nature: A Symphony of Plants, http://www.fujisan-net.gr.jp/english/4_02.htm
2. Shizuoka Prefecture: What's Mt. Fuji? http://www.pref.shizuoka.jp/a_foreign/english/fuji/whatfuji.html
3. *Charm of Mount Fuji: The Flora and Fauna Encountered in the National Parks,* http://www.yamanashi-kankou.jp/kokuritsukoen/en/ranger/doshokubutsu.html
4. Ibid.
5. Fujisan.net, Mt Fuji's Nature, Mysterious Groundwater Springs, http://www.fujisan-net.gr.jp/english/4_05.htm
6. Discovery Atlas, *Short Stories: Japan Revealed,* (Discovery Education Video)
7. Go Japan Go: Fuji-Q High Land, Fujiyoshida, http://www.gojapango.com/travel/japan.php?poi_id=668
8. Fujiyoshida Museum of Local History, http://www.city.fujiyoshida.yamanashi.jp/div/english/html/museum.html
9. Hitachi Environmental Networks: "What Is the Reverdin's Blue?" http://www.hitachi.com/environment/showcase/employee/ecosystem/fuji/01.html
10. Michihito Watanabe, "Butterflies of Mount Fuji," Earthwatch Institute Field Report, http://www.earthwatch.org/FieldReportpdf/Watanabe_FieldReport2008.pdf
11. Hitachi Environmental Networks, "Curious Relationship Between the Reverdin's Blue and Ants," http://www.hitachi.com/environment/showcase/employee/ecosystem/fuji/02.html

Chapter Five: Beloved Fuji-san

1. Mt. Fuji's Cultural Values: Wellspring of Art and Culture, Mt Fuji in Literature, http://www.mtfuji.or.jp/en/cultural_values/art_culture/03.html
2. Tracy Dahlby, "Fuji," *National Geographic,* August 2002, p. 26.
3. "Volcano Myths and Legends—Japan," Oregon State University, http://volcano.oregonstate.edu/oldroot/legends/japan/japan.html

Books

Bouquillard, Jocelyn. *Hokusai's Mount Fuji: The Complete Views in Color.* New York: Harry N. Abrams, 2007.

Florence, Debbi Michiko. *Japan: Over 40 Activities to Experience Japan—Past and Present.* Danbury, CT: Williamson Books, 2009.

Leavitt, Amie Jane. *Anatomy of a Volcanic Eruption.* Mankato, MN: Capstone Press, 2012.

Marsh, Carol. *The Mystery at Mount Fuji: Tokyo, Japan (Around the World in 80 Mysteries).* Atlanta, GA: Gallopade International, 2007.

Morley, Catherine Weyerhaeuser. *"Where Do Mountains Come From, Mama?"* Missoula, MT: Mountain Press Publishing Company, 2011.

Schreiber, Anne. *Volcanoes!* Washington, DC: National Geographic Children's Books, 2008.

Works Consulted

Dahlby, Tracy. "Fuji." *National Geographic,* August 2002.

Dahlby, Tracy. "Mount Fuji: An Iconic Peak and Trek." Cnn.com, Budget Travel Online, March 30, 2007. http://www.cnn.com/2007/TRAVEL/DESTINATIONS/03/30/mt.fuji/index.html

Fujisan.net. Mt Fuji's Nature: A Symphony of Plants. http://www.fujisan-net.gr.jp/english/4_02.htm

Fujiyoshida Museum of Local History. http://www.city.fujiyoshida.yamanashi.jp/div/english/html/museum.html

Hitachi Environmental Networks. "Curious Relationship Between the Reverdin's Blue and Ants." http://www.hitachi.com/environment/showcase/employee/ecosystem/fuji/02.html

"Mt. Fuji Climb: Yoshida Trail from Kawaguchiko." *Tokyo Times,* July 7, 2010. http://www.tokyotimes.com/post/en/1191/Mt+Fuji+Climb+Yoshida+Trail+from+Kawaguchiko.html

"Mount Fuji." Frommer's. http://www.frommers.com/destinations/tokyo/0085020381.html

Mount Fuji Volcanic Hazard Map. http://www.city.fujiyoshida.yamanashi.jp/div/bosai/html/hazard_map/q_and_a.html

"The Tragic Tale of Sir Rutherford Alcock's Dog." http://www.takaoclub.com/alcock/index.htm

"Volcanoes of Japan." Oregon State University. http://volcano.oregonstate.edu/book/export/html/368

"Volcano Myths and Legends—Japan." Oregon State University. http://volcano.oregonstate.edu/oldroot/legends/japan/japan.html

Watanabe, Michihito. "Butterflies of Mount Fuji." Earthwatch Institute Field Report. http://www.earthwatch.org/FieldReportpdf/Watanabe_FieldReport2008.pdf

Welcome to Japan: National Parks, Fuji-Hakone-Izu National Park. http://www.welcome-to.jp/nationalparks/Fuji.html

Yates, Ronald E. "Mt Fuji Climbers Find Its Grandeur Slipping." *Chicago Tribune,* March 24, 1986. http://articles.chicagotribune.com/1986-03-24/news/8601210974_1_fuji-volcanic-ash-mt

Yoshida's Fire Festival, Fujiyoshida City Official Web Site. http://www.city.fujiyoshida.yamanashi.jp/div/english/html/firefest.html

On the Internet

Children's Encyclopedia, Mount Fuji
http://kids.britannica.com/elementary/article-353157/Mount-Fuji

Kids Web Japan
http://web-jpn.org/kidsweb/explore/nature/q1.html

National Geographic Education: Ring of Fire
http://education.nationalgeographic.com/education/encyclopedia/ring-fire/?ar_a=1

National Geographic Find People and Places, Japan
http://kids.nationalgeographic.com/kids/places/find/japan/

National Geographic, Mount Fuji
http://video.nationalgeographic.com/video/kids/people-places-kids/japan-mtfuji-kids/

Time for Kids, Japan
http://www.timeforkids.com/destination/japan

convergent (KUN-ver-jint) **plate boundary**—Site where two land plates meet and push together.

core—The center of the earth.

deity (DEE-uh-tee)—A god.

divergent (dy-VER-jint) **plate boundary**—Site where two land plates pull apart.

endangered (en-DAYN-jurd)—A species of plants or animals that are decreasing drastically in population size.

extinct (EKS-tinkt)—A species that used to exist; a species whose entire population has died out.

lava—Hot, liquid rock that flows out of the earth's crust.

magma—Hot, liquid rock in the mantle (middle) of the earth.

mantle (MAN-tuhl)—The part of the earth that is just below the crust and contains liquid rock (magma).

plate boundary—A place where two of the earth's plates (or pieces of crust) meet.

shrine—A special place where people go to worship gods.

souvenir (SOO-vuh-neer)—An object that a person purchases or obtains from a visited place to keep as a memory.

stratovolcano (STRAT-oh-vall-KAY-noh)—A volcano built up of alternating layers of lava and ash.

summit—The top of a mountain.

tectonic (tek-TAH-nik) **plates**—Pieces of the earth's crust.

torii (TOHR-ee)—A wooden arch that marks the entrance of a Shinto shrine.

treeline—The place on a mountain (at a certain elevation) where trees are unable to grow.

volatile (VAH-luh-tul)—Explosive; tendency to erupt.

About the AUTHOR

Amie Jane Leavitt is an accomplished author, researcher, and photographer. She graduated from Brigham Young University as an education major and has since taught all subjects and grade levels in both private and public schools. Leavitt is an adventurer who loves to travel the globe in search of interesting story ideas and beautiful places to capture in photos. She has written more than fifty books for kids, has contributed to online and print media, and has worked as a consultant, writer, and editor for numerous educational publishing and assessment companies. When Leavitt was in high school, she had the opportunity to take three years of Japanese for her foreign language credits. Since that time, she has held a great love for Japanese people and culture. Because of that, she thoroughly enjoyed both researching and writing this book on Mount Fuji. To see a list of Leavitt's current projects and published works, visit her web site at http://www.amiejaneleavitt.com.